From Butterflies to Caterpillars

By: Tatiana Whigham

From Butterflies to Caterpillars

Copyright © 2016 by **Tatiana Whigham**. All rights reserved.

No part of this publication may be reproduced, stored in a retrieval system or transmitted in any way by any means, electronic, mechanical, photocopy, recording or otherwise, without the prior permission of the author except as provided by USA copyright law.

All characters appearing in this work are fictitious. Any resemblance to real persons, living or dead, is purely coincidental.

The opinions expressed by the author are not necessarily those of Revival Waves of Glory Books & Publishing.

Published by Revival Waves of Glory Books & Publishing
PO Box 596| Litchfield, Illinois 62056 USA
www.revivalwavesofgloryministries.com

Revival Waves of Glory Books & Publishing is committed to excellence in the publishing industry.

Book design Copyright © 2016 by Revival Waves of Glory Books & Publishing. All rights reserved.

Published in the United States of America

Paperback: 978-0692707104

Table of Contents

Introduction 4

Chapter 1 8

Chapter 2 19

Chapter 3 36

Chapter 4 44

Chapter 5 53

Chapter 6 58

Other Books By Tatiana Whigham 60

INTRODUCTION

Queens, New York

March 17, 2013

Taja

"Hey, are you going to stand there all day or are you going to bat already?"

"I'm coming, I'm coming," I say, swatting flies all the way from the dugout. Coach Willis has this rule that at practice, every member of the team has to go to bat before leaving for the day. Man, I really think that this league is for everyone, because I suck. I mean, for real though. No pun intended. Even though I try my best to hide out and be one of the last ones (hoping to be forgotten), he still makes me bat knowing that I would be bad at it. I guess it's safe to say that sports aren't for everybody.

"Any day now," yells Kathleen, the leading pitcher on our team. And despite her taunting ways, she's actually pretty good. She's one of the best players in Queens that I've seen yet. I mean, who's ever seen a 13 year-old throw 65-80 mph pitches. Just the thought of it is insane.

"Alright Kathleen! Give me time." As I near the plate, I do my best to get into batter's position. Let's see: knees bent, butt out, elbows up, and face the pitcher. I was never really taught how to correctly choose which side of the plate to bat from, so I stand on the right side simply because everyone else does.

"Ready?"

"Don't I look it?" Norma, who's currently playing catcher, tries her hardest to muffle a laugh. I glance at her with a snob-eyed look that reads, 'please, don't tempt me!' It only takes seconds for me to realize that she understands, because before I know it, she's straightened her face guard and has gotten back into the catcher position. Glancing back at Kathleen, I assure her that I'm ready.

As she whines back, I prepare myself for the killer, and in that instance it happens.

Papp!

"Strike One." Darn it the luck. I completely flaked on that pitch. But not willing to let one pitch deter me, I get back into position.

"Come on Taja, I know two year-olds who can swing better than that!" exclaims Kathleen as she tickles herself funny on the pitcher's mound. I back off of the plate, shaking my head, as she struggles to pull herself together. She laughs so loud and hard that half of the team follows suit. With all of this anger on the inside of me, if God don't hold me, I don't know what will. Man, I told momma not to sign me up. But no, according to her, every child in her house has to be doing something, and I don't have any problems with that. I'm glad to get out of the house most of the time, but not for this. She could've easily picked the chess team, the book club, or even the math club. Why in God's name did she have to pick softball?

Looking up, it's clear that Kathleen is still strung out on the giggles. I swear the next ball I hit is going straight for her mouth. She's always got something to say.

"Taja, come on. We have other people waiting to bat," shouts Coach Willis, interrupting my thoughts. One would think that he would at least try to stop the other girls from laughing. But no, he's too busy tampering with his iPhone. You see, City Hall dumps loads of money into companies who donate their time during the year with leisure services, because according to them (and I quote) 'Our Children are Our Future.' But here's the problem with that, most of the people volunteering know absolutely nothing about the sport or working with children for that matter. So in my eyes, it would do us more justice to coach ourselves, but who would listen to a bunch of 11 & 13 year-olds? Feeling thoroughly defeated, I reposition myself at the batter's plate anyway.

"Ok Coach."

Kathleen winds up again, as if she's really ready to play. One . . . two. . . . Wait for it. . . .

I see it; it's almost here. I'm gripping the bat, ready for the swing and . . .

Papp!

"Strike two!" cries Norma. As the words leave her mouth, I can faintly hear the murmur of giggles from the other players patrolling the bases. I look up to Coach Willis for some support or even help, but he's already turned his back arguing with someone on the other end of the phone. All I can do is shake my head. "It figures."

"You know, I might as well throw anything, because you're never going to swing. Ha! Ha!" The laughter that comes from her and the others has become more audible now.

"Shut up Kathleen."

"Oh! Are we mad already?" She teases, doing her best to mock me. And the ring of laughter envelops yet again.

"I'm going to hit the next one, just you wait." I angrily get back into position, tapping the plate to assure her that I'm ready. But this time, I step too close. She winds up, still laughing, but surprisingly, she manages to throw the pitch.

Smack!

The ball hits me dead in my left eye and like a feather tossed in the wind, I hit the ground. Holding my hands in front of my face, all I see is blood on my hands. Crying from both the pain and the sight of the blood (which seems to run faster by the minute), I cry out with a voice so loud that even I forget that it's me. With tears in one eye and blood in the other, I cry and squirm on the ground mixing the dirt with my bloody tears. With everyone now surrounding me, all I hear are the screams which happen to be coming from me.

CHAPTER 1

August 5, 2013

Taja

It's like jumping into the sea with no air to breathe, and being suffocated while others are still watching me. Trying to stand in sinking sand is like trying to catch fish on another's dry land. Until you've felt the pain and sorrow, please don't you dare question me about tomorrow. You see, I'm trying to explain to you the way that I feel. There's no reason to second guess, I'm just trying to keep it real. I'm 11 years old and I've lost my sight in all but one eye. Now I have to learn how to live within the chains of being disabled which feels worse than a baby being caged in a cradle. Lord, Lord, what shall become of me . . . the blind man who once did see.

During my 6th grade orientation, I walk through the halls alongside my mom and a counselor appearing just as lost as can be. Not only am I starting junior high, but I'll be starting the year off as a new enrollee in the disability program here at St. Johnson Middle. I promise you, this year can't get any more embarrassing. Just a few months back, I was normal and able. Now it's August, and everyone is treating me like I'm five minutes from being mentally retarded. According to this new what's-her-face, I have to be escorted everywhere I go. I can't attend normal classes, because due to my new found 'situation,' I have to have a person assisting me at all times. Really? I have to show up for lunch everyday 15-30 minutes early with the 'specially challenged'. I mean, I'm the most normal person in the group, and that's not saying much. Just a few months ago, I was picked to be inducted into the honor's program, and now I'm here.

Finally circling our way back to the disability office, Ms. What's-her-face turns toward us and says, "Well, that's the end of the tour. Do you have any questions?"

"Oh, no ma'am you've answered all of mine. Turning toward me, momma asks, "Sweetie, what about you?". Not really feeling it, I put my head down. It's a shame, my toes will have more freedom than me.

Feeling my disconnect, the counselor (aka Ms. What's-her-face) carries on with the conversation. "Well that settles it then. I'm sure that Taja will adjust fairly quickly to the new routine. And as always, we'll be available if she needs us. Again, my name is Ms. Martha. My doors are open anytime for both you and Taja. So with that being said, welcome to St. Johnson."

"Thank you ma'am. We look forward to working with you. Have a nice day," says momma in her most 'I-really-care' voice.

"Alright, we'll be in touch. Take care." And with a wave, Ms. What's-her-face (who I now know to be Ms. Martha) walks off, and my mom and I are on our way.

Judging by her fast pace, I just know that I am in for it when we get to the car. And once again, I was right. Momma yanks me by the collar and swirls me in front of her all in one motion.

"Dear Jesus child, what is the matter with you? The school, the doctors, me, we're all doing our best to help you through this, but what's the use if you're not even willing to try?" Now nose-to-nose with me, momma looks as if my mere silence makes her madder by the minute. Squeezing my arm with the death grip, she yanks me again, even harder this time. "Answer me! Answer me! Do you hear me talking to you?"

With tears rolling down my face at a constant speed, I try my best to muffle a simple 'yes ma'am,' but all that comes out is an over toned cry. So caught up in our own actions, we're completely oblivious to the fact that we have incurred an audience (parents, students, and teachers stand in shock at the whole ordeal). Before I can answer, I see a hand touching my mom's shoulder. It's Ms. Martha. Realizing the attention that she's attracted, my mom straightens up and prepares to talk her way out of the already terrifying situation.

"Ma'am, I do believe that that is enough."

"Oh, well I was just talking with my daughter about the importance of being appreciative. Wasn't I sweetie?" asks my mom, looking to me with a look that reads, 'you-better- say-yes.'

Feeling the tension, Ms. Martha intervenes, "Well ma'am that's great. I know that situations like this can be frustrating, but we have to remember to stay positive. Whether you believe it or not, this is actually a difficult process for your daughter."

"Look ma'am, Ms. Martha is it?" says my mom, as she swallows hard before her next sentence. "I'm perfectly capable of taking care of my daughter, and I don't need some two-by-four, blonde haired pig-face woman trying to tell me how to handle MY DAUGHTER. Believe me, I got this!" yells momma. Witnessing a glimpse of momma's temper-tantrum, two of the school officers ease their way through the crowd and stand guard behind Ms. Martha.

Realizing that she's now outnumbered, momma decides to cut the conversation short, "You know what; I don't have time for this." Opening the car door, she demands, "Get in Taja."

"Ma'am, I really don't think."

Jumping out of the front seat in lieu of her anger, "Did I ask you what you thought? Did I?"

"Well no, but ma'am…"

"No, no I didn't. So let me tell you what you're going to do. You're going to take your little high-tail self back in there and let me do what I do best. I'm a parent, so I'm going to do a parent's job regardless of what you're busy 'thinking'."

"Ma'am, as an advocate for children and their safety, I can't let you leave with this child. Not in this state of emotion."

"Please!" momma yells, turning around thoroughly ignoring the counselor. "Taja, get in the car."

"Taja, do not get in the car," cautions Ms. Martha. Then she turns to momma, "Ma'am, I strongly…"

"Taja! Taja! Get in the car!"

"Come here sweetie," coaxes Ms. Martha. Seeing momma yelling like a mad woman, I really don't know what to do. But with Ms. Martha reaching for me with her arms stretched out wide, I unconsciously begin to walk toward her. At least I know that she's not going to beat me.

Starring in shock, momma jumps out of the car, slams the door, and lunges at Ms. Martha like an angry beast that's been caged for some time. As momma tackles Ms. Martha to the ground, the officers go straight for her. As they drag her, kicking and screaming, my heart races and my legs begin to move, far, far away. I don't know where but my legs continue to move far, far away. And with all of the commotion, no one sees . . . no one cares. . . .When they finally look up, I'll be long gone from here. Into the bushes behind the school, my feet continue to make paths through the woods.

***

Chicago, Illinois

Nicki

As the night time comes, I can feel the gentle breeze. To some, that means it's time to go in and go to sleep. To me, it means that it's time to rustle up enough cash to make it through the week. As I slip on my heels, one shoe at a time, visions *of my reality come to mind. Glancing in the mirror at the reflection looking back at me, I wonder, am I too skinny? Is my face too small? Or are the hopes of my future just way too tall? On with the mascara, the eye shadow, and yes, my lips are aligned. It's crazy that I'm living this way all of the time. Checking my frame, I can hike my dress up here and there. Flipping the flat iron, I'm making curls everywhere. Who is this girl smiling back at me? She seems to show up every night of the week. To some, this girl has fallen from quite a spiritual height. But to me, it's not fantasy, it's just plain life.*

"Nicki, girl what are you staring at? You've been looking at yourself for about ten minutes already." Turning from the mirror, I crack a smile at my best friend, Jenna. Jenna's maybe 5'5, with brown eyes, and a model-like vibe (well, a plus-size one anyway). Though she's a mother of two by day and a street walker by night, she's still one of the sweetest people that I've ever meet in my life.

"Now you know I got to be right." Doing my best pose, I turn to her again, "What do you think? Too much?"

Coming toward the mirror, Jenna stands beside me. "Girl, it's way too much. You're not going to get anybody standing up there looking high-yellow desperate."

"Uhhhh. . . You know what, I give up," I say, sounding thoroughly frustrated. Though I've only been doing this gig for a few weeks, I still haven't mastered it. Who knew that selling sex on the street would take this much practice?

"Girl ok, this is nothing like that strip club that you used to dance at with loud music and dim lights. You have to look the part and believe it. Remember, no one is buying you, they're buying their fantasy." Jenna moves behind me and places her hands on my tense shoulders. "You have to relax, take a deep breath, and play the part. You can't level with these people, because nobody is buying you. No one cares that you're from North Philly, no one cares that you spent two years in some Ivy League school, no one cares that you paint in your private time . . . no one cares. Most of these men are coming from dead-end marriages, stressful relationships, high-end jobs, or they're just pure victims of the streets. They want something that they can control and harness; not something that they have to work at. You're just fantasy remember. . . .Their fantasy... Now, are you ready?"

"Yeah, I am." And with that, we gather our jackets and purses and make our way to the door. But before leaving, I glance back at the mirror, "Well, Chi-town here we come." And with that, we're off, the infamous ladies of the night.

The night goes on like any other. Jenna and I are freelancers, so we keep 100% of our earnings. But it still doesn't amount to much, because we're banned from the most popular spots which are guarded by the hustlers collecting their money. If we even step foot on the North-Side, East and Lane, or Carnell Drive, we'd have to give 45% up front to whoever runs that joint. And living from night to night as is, that's just a cut I'm not willing to take. So Jenna and I travel Parten-Way, a middle-upper class roadway. Traffic here is much slower, but the customers pay decent enough. The Army base isn't too far from here (maybe 30 minutes to an hour), and those boys are always ready to party. Not to mention the truckers and regular pedestrians passing along the way. It's not in the heart of Chicago, but it's close enough for us anyway. With restaurants, bars, and clubs lining the streets, we always have places to rest our feet. But in these places, the way you dress means everything. You have to look the part, but not dress like it, cause these cops up here will get you quick. They travel the streets on horses up here. So up here, black-on-black is the code of the streets. Tonight, I put on black, high heel boots, a red mini-dress, topped off with a black trench coat. In weather like this, you really can't tell whether I'm dressed for business or pleasure, unless of course you know the streets. Jenna's a little more fearless than I am. She's always going to be her regardless of where she's at, and people respect her for it. She's a woman of many talents. She'll walk the streets for an hour or two, and the next minute you see her, she'll be on stage singing at some club or bartending behind somebody else's counter. I, on the other hand, am not as blessed, so I usually just follow her lead. She has on a black mini-dress, black heels, and a black jacket, always carrying a cigarette in one hand and a drink in the other.

Posted up talking and laughing, we're caught up in our own world – a world that crowds never see. In the midst of our conversation, high beams pull up slowing to a complete stop. Curious, we watch as the tinted windows cruise downward. "Hey sweet thang," a familiar face sits up in the driver's seat. It's Roy, one of Jenna's regulars. Jenna leans forward, nearing the window and smiles back at him.

"Well, what did you have in mind?" breathes Jenna just as calm and cool as can be.

"You tell me," he replies, letting down the rest of the windows in the car revealing the other three passengers who are obviously looking for a good time. "How about you and your girl come ride with us?"

Smiling in agreement, Jenna turns and looks at me. However, seeing the look of distain on my face, she stands up, and turns to Roy, "Give us a minute to freshen up for you baby."

He cracks a grin, and smirks, "Sounds good to me."

Jenna takes me to the restroom of the bar directly behind our post. "Girl, what is the matter with you? That's four dudes in one night, two for you and two for me. What's the deal?"

"I just . . . I just don't feel right about it. If it was one guy maybe, but with four you never know what's on their minds."

"Are you crazy? You know Roy. I know Roy. He's good people, not to mention that he pays well. Night's like this they probably just got paid and are looking to have a good time. What's wrong with that?"

"Yeah, but…"

"But what?" Taking a step back now, she throws a sly grin my way. "Oh, I see what this is. You're too good for something like this aren't you?"

"I didn't say that."

"You didn't have too. Look, whatever is going through your mind right now, you need to cut it out. Bottom line, you have bills to pay and your own mouth to feed." Grabbing her purse and heading for the door, "It's your call. But as for me, I'm going to make this paper." and with that, she slams the door behind her.

Taking a minute to let this all soak in, I stand in front of the mirror looking at the reflection staring back at me. The girl in the mirror seems to be crying blinded tears in an empty space where there's no one to hear.

"I HATE YOU, I HATE YOU!" I scream, banging the mirror with everything in me, trying to erase the image that I see. But after all of that, she's still there staring back at me through the cracked glass. Tired and frustrated, I pick up the trash can and hurl it at the mirror shattering the glass to mere pieces. Still crying, I lean against the hard wall and its coolness is the only comfort to me.

Knock! Knock! Knock!

"Ma'am, is everything ok?" Knock! Knock! "Ma'am?"

Knock! Knock!

Feeling the call of the wild yet again, I stand up, for real this time. I gather my belongings and head for the door.

Knock! Knock!

"Ma'am? Ma'am, are you ok?"

Opening the door, I stare at the woman standing in the doorway, "No . . . but I'm going to be."

And with that, I walk past her. Seconds later, apparently having seen the damage in the bathroom, I hear a faint yell, "Ma'am, Ma'am." But it's too late; I already have a date with reality.

Exiting the bar, I see Jenna standing against the car talking with Roy. With one look at me, horror comes across her face. Seeing my messed up hair, mascara trails written in my own tears, and my bloody hands, she moves toward me, "Nicki what happened?"

"Life." Feeling free, I smile at her as I turn to go the opposite way . . . my way, down the streets, through the crowd where no one notices me, no one sees, no one cares.

"Nicki, Nicki!" I can faintly hear Jenna calling for me in the background, but it's too late. I'm already gone.

CHAPTER 2

Queens, New York

February 17, 2014

Taja

Rustle trees rustle, fall leaves fall, sometimes it's best to sit and wait after all. I tried to run from the hurt and the pain, only to be brought back into this broken frame. A frame that once held life and opportunity, now only serves as a picture of the things that have been lost to me. Momma got arrested for being a poor choice of a role model. So she, being bound and gagged, was dragged by the police officers and made to follow. Mrs. Martha, on the other hand, rests with no end trying to find me a new home. But no matter where I go, I always feel so alone. Blind in one eye, struggling to see, it's like I'm fighting a losing battle while trying to be seen. Seen for the goodness, that I know that I harbor, but until someone finds it, I must be termed Sorrow's Daughter.

Beep! Beep!

While standing at the curb, patiently waiting for my ride, this beige SUV pulls up with some lady honking her horn like there's no tomorrow.

Beep! Beep!

Judging from the look of things, it must be my new foster mom. Man, why do they always do that? These fosters sure are a trip. It's just so embarrassing; I mean, you don't have to honk your horn a million times for me to see you. They talk extra loud like I've lost my hearing too. They follow me around like I'm going to trip and fall over my own two feet, and they constantly hover like some nut off of Dr. Phil.

Beep! Beep!

I turn to see the smiling face through the front windshield, which happens to be some oldie-goldie who's waving like a maniac. Everyone on the curb starts to laugh. I mean good grief, you're the third car in line already. At least wait until you reach the pick-up stop.

"Tell me that old hag isn't waiting for you?" smirks Kathleen as everyone else begins to laugh even harder. I tell you, a new school year and all, and she's still the same.

"Shut your mouth, fish-eyes."

"Make me, you blind-bat! But it's cool. I mean, I'd be mad too if I had to walk around all day like blind Sallie-Sue," trying her best to taunt me, she playfully walks around like some blind person on cane. Oh my mistake, I guess that poor shot of a performance is supposed to be me. What a joke! With everything in me, I quickly throw two hard-bound textbooks in her direction. Catching her off guard, one of the books obviously makes contact and she hits the floor. The fight is on!

"Fight! Fight!" yells someone in the crowd.

I give her two quick jabs to the face and quickly move to pin her. Poor girl, she's so disoriented that she can barely return a punch. "Now how's that for a blind bat, you old fish-eyed fool."

Within seconds, I feel someone lifting me like a sack of groceries. Anxious to finish what I started, I'm kicking and screaming the whole way. And judging from the looks of things, a few of my kicks hit the target dead on. "Who's the dummy now?"

Pushing me against the car, a woman bends down in front of me. It takes me a few seconds to realize that this is the same woman from the SUV.

"My Lord child, what's the matter with you? Fighting like this is some hoe-down or something." Taking a second to let her words sink in, she stands up. "Now, you're Taja, aren't you? Taja Graham? My name is Mrs. Patterson. You'll call me Mrs. Patterson. You might as well get all of that foolish out of your system right now, because it ain't coming home with me." Pulling me to the passenger door of her SUV, she motions for me to get in and I do. Closing the door behind me, she goes back to the curb to retrieve my bag and my books. And with that we're off. Welcome to my new life.

The vehicle itself seems to be somewhat spotless, which could only me one thing, this woman is some sort of neat freak, where everything has to look perfect and everything has to be put in its right place. While riding, some chic erupts on the radio,

"When everything goes wrong, you see some bad. But I'm just a soul whose intentions are good. Oh Lord, please don't let me be misunderstood..."

"Oh child, that's old folks music right there. Don't you just love that rhythm?" asks Mrs. Patterson as she turns toward me from the driver's seat, obviously reading my thoughts. "It's called '*Don't Let Me Be Misunderstood.*' That's Nina Simone, a true songstress of the heart. No matter what song you play of hers, you can feel yourself in all of 'em; with every word so on point, and every thought so powerfully clear. I tell you, God only gives people special talent to do that. Don't you think?" she asks, turning towards me in expectation. Having much rather listen to the song with its cool jazz melody, I turn and face my window instead, hoping to get lost amidst the verses.

". . .I'm just human. Don't you know that I have faults like anyone? Sometimes I find myself alone regretting, some little foolish thing. Some simple thing that I've done. . ."

Pulling to a stop, the radio dies out and we enter life yet again. Getting out of the car, I look up at a building that I've seen many times before, the Queens' Courthouse. The very place where hope ends and life begins. Walking in, I know the procedure. I sit in the hallway of children's services and wait for the foster parent to come out with the documentation. This time is no different. As Mrs. Patterson goes into the office, I take to my own thoughts. Gosh this place really needs an upgrade. With white walls, pale floors, and these forget-me-not chairs, it looks to be every bit of an insane asylum. Right across the hall is the office for the Women's Shelter. People go in there to hide out from abuse, get off of the streets, or simply just to receive free assistance. Their line in the hallway is always jam packed, but today, they only have one person in line. She could be somewhat pretty but with her hair all in a mess, clothes just as dingy as ever (like they haven't seen a washing machine in months), and all out trashy sort of vibe, it's hard to tell whether she's going or coming.

Feeling me staring at her, she offers up conversation in her own defense. "Hey."

"Hey."

"Ain't you ever seen a stranger before child?"

"Yeah . . . but my momma said not to talk to them."

"Oh really?" giggles the woman obviously amused. "Well, don't you ever listen?"

"Sometimes."

"What's your name?"

"Taja."

"I'm Nicki. So, uh, was that your mom that just went in?"

"No."

"Your grandma?"

"My mom's gone." The silence that follows is deafening, Feeling as if it's my turn to take over the conversation, I say the only thing that comes to mind. . ., "You should probably put on some shoes."

She looks down at her bare feet, free to feel the naked air. "Oh, well I had some, but they hurt too badly, so I had to take them off."

"You stand a lot?"

"Why you ask?"

"Momma says that her feet hurt a lot when she stands up and works all day. That's why she's tired when she gets home."

"Oh . . . that sounds about right."

At that exact moment, out comes Mrs. Patterson with papers in hand. "Alright child, I guess that settles it," she exclaims, motioning for me to follow her. Before leaving, I sneak a wave to the young lady sitting in the chair. She smiles and waves back. And out the door we go.

As we crank up and head out, Nina Simone's rhythmic voice blasts through the speakers.

". . .Cause I'm just a soul whose intentions are good. Oh Lord, Please don't let me be misunderstood. Don't let me be misunderstood. I try so hard. So please don't let me be misunderstood. . ."

****

March 02, 2014

Nicki

Oh I'm feeling the crazy weather in these city streets. Some days are hot and wet, while others are dry and cold. Dear Lord, please don't dismiss me as something old. When I left Chicago, I thought that I'd left my troubles too. But with no funds and an empty stomach, I had to find something to do. I hitched-hiked rides all the way to Queens, only to find out that even people here are ruthless and mean. So I connected with this guy who claimed to be my missing piece, but he only wanted to use the parts of me that he could see. My hips, my thighs, and my bright brown eyes were again being sold for simple fantasies and little *lies. Unable to sustain, I had to find some way to cope. So I ended up on the streets strung out on dope. It's been a true struggle trying to break free. I'm beginning to question whether or not it's worth saving me. I even went to this shelter, this center here in town, only to find out that there was no help to be found. No one wants to save a strung out prostitute. Dear Lord, now what do I do?*

After chugging my last glass of Rum & Coke, I shift my lace front, powder my face, and prepare myself for the night ahead of me. One thing I can say, folks up here sure are taken by street love. I've been through three guys tonight and it's only 7pm. Pretty good, huh? I wonder how Jenna is doing. I haven't spoken to her in a while, but it was time for a change.

"Thanks Jim," I say, waving at the bartender on my way out.

"Anytime. Be careful out there."

"Will do." I reply, as I enter the crowd of nameless faces. People out here sell anything on the streets: sex, weave, drugs, baked goods, and so on. I mean the works. I walk the streets smiling at the faces eying me, all the while trying to escape reality. Then I spot him, some jazz cat coming out of Zoe's Diner dressed in black slacks, a reddish-black tie, and a black buttoned up top. Dressed like that, he can't be from around here, but at least he looks like he'll pay well.

"Hey good looking, headed my way?"

After taking a sip of his drink, he manages to speak, "Maybe, maybe not."

"Ahhh, wouldn't that be a shame?" I ask, now leaning against the wall beside him, doing my getcha-gotcha pose (butt out, leg up).

Turning back towards the streets, he pulls out the keys to his car and unlocks it from where he stands. Walking to the vehicle, he opens the passenger door and turns to me, "If you're looking for a good time, I believe that I can help you with that."

Got him! With a sexy smile and killer walk, I climb into his truck (an all-black SUV with black tinted windows, and smooth black leather seats). Closing my door behind me, I get the impression that he must be a gentleman. And I'm glad, because the last three were anything short of senseless, I promise you. As he gets into the truck, his features become clearer to me. Dark skin, clean cut, and no wedding ring, you've got to be kidding me. He looks to be a few years short of thirty, which is good because that means that he's probably mature and well-mannered. As we drive off into the distance, the silence is killing me. I'm way too drank and high to sit here and not say a word, so I calmly and coolly turn towards him, "So what's on your mind?"

"Nothing much."

"Are you going to tell me where we're headed?" Choosing not to respond, he just looks at me and smiles. Ok, now I'm confused . . . and a little freaked-out.

"Name's Terrell." As he extends his hand to mine, which I shake in a greeting gesture. "And you are?"

"Nickemma Hines, but I go by Nicki." Most guys that I deal with aren't interested in me, let alone my name.

We've been riding for about five minutes now and he hasn't even made a pass at me yet. I hope he knows that this comes with the job; I mean, you don't have to work your way in, that's kind of the point.

"You cold?" He reaches in the back seat and grabs his top coat and with his free hand places it over my legs. "There you go."

Shocked and thoroughly not sure of what to do, I manage to smile and say, "Thanks, I guess." You know most guys wouldn't find a mini skirt, heels, and a halter top offensive. Who does this guy think he is? If I wanted a wardrobe rearrangement or some 'you should do better about yourself lecture' I wouldn't be out here now would I? His mannerisms and gestures are quickly ticking me off. I just want to do whatever we're going to do and be done already. I've got things to do and people to see, so let's keep it moving.

Sensing my irritation, he turns to me with a Bernie Sanders Kool-Aid smile, "We're here."

Looking up at the place in front of us, I ask, "Is this a joke?"

Shaking his head, he replies, "No, not at all." His eyes were set on me probably enjoying my reaction.

"This is a church."

"You said that you wanted a good time. This week's revival, we have some awesome guest speakers, praise and worship, of course dinner afterwards and--"

"I don't care about no darn speakers and worship. I'm not walking in there. Is this supposed to be like some funny jack in the box trick, or some--"

"No!"

"Then what is it?"

"I just thought . . . I just thought that at this point, you need a word more than anything."

Looking stunned with my mouth wide opened, "I'll tell you what I need right now, to get far away from you." Jumping out of the vehicle, I begin to charter the streets. I'm a few blocks out, but I guess I can find my way back.

"Hey, wait a minute," he shouts, running behind me. "Hey, can you wait you?"

Finally catching up to me, he says, "I mean, what's so wrong with going to church."

"I don't need some lecture and some 'I can do better speech' from somebody like you."

"Like me?"

"Yes, like you."

"You don't even know me."

"I know enough, and the last thing I need is for somebody to be judging me all because I'm not living in God's Will and crap…"

"Whooooo, no one's judging you alright. I just. . I just…" stumbling through his words, he tries his hardest to regain my attention. "You know what. Forget this."

thoroughly frustrated, he digs into his pockets. "How much do you charge an hour?"

"What?"

"How much?"

"You can't afford me."

"Try me."

Embarrassed to tell him my real rate of $30, I decide to up the scales. He looks like he can afford it, "$100".

"Ok, service usually lasts about two hours and we have dinner afterwards, so here's $250." He pushes the money in my face. Half in shock, I'm not really sure what to do.

"Are you serious?"

"As a heart attack."

There's no need of letting money like this go to waste, so I take it. It would have taken me almost two nights to raise this, so . . . . Thank you Jesus. "Alright two hours it is and not a minute after."

"Sounds good to me."

And that's how I entered the house of the Lord for the first time in over seven years. Lord have mercy on me.

As we enter the church, the ushers dressed in white meet us at the door with programs reading 'Welcome to Mt. Calvary's 15th annual church revival.' Walking the aisle seems embarrassing enough, with the church packed and all. I have to be the only one with a skirt above my knees, a back-out shirt top, and a curly wig. Not wanting to turn the heads of too many people, I jet for the first free slot in the back of the church that I can find.

Just as I move to claim my seat, Terrell grabs my arm gently lifting me up as he leans over to me, "You think that I'm going to let you sit here, so that you can leave at will. No, you're coming with me." Seeing how uncomfortable I am, he again gives me his top coat. "Here you go."

"Thank you." As we walk down the aisle, heads turn whispering to one another. Seeing this, Terrell holds my hand. He was right about one thing though, the praise and worship is awesome. When we walked in, the choir was singing '*He's a Battle Axe.*' Now deep in worship, they're singing '*Way Back*'.

"...Me and Jesus, we go a long way back. Me and Jesus, we go a long way back. Long, long, long, long waaaaay.... waaaaay back..."

As we finally reach our seats on the second row, I'm so excited to sit down. The lady on my left, who's been eyeing me since I reached the seat, scoots over as if my apparel is about to taint her praise, but I don't mind though. It's praises like this that make me think back to when I was little. Being the daughter of a preacher, it was mandatory for me to show up to every service. We used to have the type of revivals and shut-ins that would make you feel like Jesus was coming quick, fast, and in a hurry. But as I grew, I saw first-hand how trifling these Christian folks can be. I tell you, church hurt is the worst, because it brings down another's self-worth.

"What did I tell you? It's good huh?" he asks, smiling with that wide Kool-Aid grin.

"Yeah, it is."

The service all in all is pretty great. To be honest, had I known that the service was going to be like this, I probably would've come on my own. Well, at least I would've thought about it.

"Praise the Lord everybody!" says the Preacher as he gears up for his message.

The congregation repeats. "Praise the Lord."

"I tell you it's truly an honor to be in the house of the Lord at least one more time. I'm not going to prolong the time, so we'll get right into it. Our text will be coming from Jonah 1: 1-4. Please stand when you have your word and say Amen." Waiting patiently, the Preacher glances over his congregation. "You know I was so honored to be invited on tonight, because right here in the heart of Queens, we as a community have some serious issues. Across the street, we have liquor stores. Two blocks down, we have prostitutes, drug addicts, and gang bangers." I slide down in my chair not really knowing what else to expect. Sensing my discomfort, Terrell grabs my hand again. "In the school houses, children bring weapons more than they bring books. And to top it off, we're all dealing with personal issues and pressures of our own. Church, we have some issues. But tonight, we're going to focus on Jonah's issues and Jonah's problems." Realizing that everyone has found their page, he proceeds "And it reads, . . ."

Not really wishing to listen to the entire four verses being read, my eyes unconsciously begin to drift from person to person. Within seconds, I spot the face, which from the looks of things has been looking at me for quite some time now. It was a familiar one. It looks like the little girl that I meet at the courthouse a few days ago, the precious little girl (whose name is Taja I believe) with no mom. Recognizing me as well, she manages to wave and so do I.

Nudging me back to reality, Terrell looks at me trying to ensure that my eyes were on the Lord. Ha! Ha! I have to thank him for an honest effort though. Turning back towards the pulpit now, the preacher is finally motioning for everyone to sit down (which in most churches is a clear indication that the scripture has been read).

". . . And my subject for tonight is, 'It's not over yet.' Many times, we are taught that Jonah ran from commitment. Jonah ran from responsibility, and Jonah ran from obligation. My Christian friends, while all of this is true, we have to be careful not to ignore the fact that Jonah wasn't just running from a duty, he was running from pressure. Everybody turn to your neighbor and say 'pressure.' You know I read in an article a little ways back, that a science teacher wanted to demonstrate to her students the pressure build-up of a volcano. So she took a 2 liter coke bottle with just a quarter full of coke and closed the lid. When she shook it once, the bottle began to tighten. When she shook it a second time, the bottle began to tighten some more. After several tries, the bottle tightened so much that the top of the bottle flew off. You see the bottle was the body, but the coke was the problem. The more that you shake up your problem (the more that you think on it, the more that you cry over it, the more that you speak over it) the more pressure, the more chaos, the more hell that it gives you. In the text, God commanded Jonah to 'Go.' The first day that God spoke this, Jonah was like 'Cool.' The next day, Jonah had begun to think on this thing, 'God told me to do what?' The day after that, Jonah had been wrestling with this thing for so long that fear and doubt began to take camp. God said 'Go,' but how many of you know that you can't move when you're weighted down. Paul says it best in 2 Corinthians 1:8, how he 'was pressed on every side, beyond measure, so that even he despaired his own life.' Somebody say pressure! Somebody has relationship pressure, financial pressure, past pressure, job pressure, family pressure, depression pressure, low self-esteem pressure, I'm-not-good-enough pressure, I-don't-have-much pressure, whatever your brand of pressure is, you have some type of 'pressure.' And when you harbor pressure for so long, it's going to become a weight on your soul. And when you're pressed, you find it hard to stand. When you're pressed, you find it hard to move forward, that's why every step you take it looks like you're going backwards, because you're pressed. When you're pressed, you're always looking back. You can't see where God is taking you, because you're too busy looking back at what's behind you. When you're pressed, you feel pressure on the left. You feel pressure on the right to the point where living, hallelujah Lord, becomes a struggle. It becomes a struggle to wake up day after day still carrying the same weight. Jonah was pressed to the point where he couldn't even walk into his destiny, couldn't even walk into his territory, couldn't even walk into his blessing. And what I like most about pressure is that it has the capability to make you fear things that will never become an issue." Pausing for a second, allowing his words to impact the congregation all the more. "Ya'll ain't with me tonight. All you're what ifs: what if I don't make it? What if I fail? What if things don't work out? . . . .What if? What if? Let me go ahead and burst your bubble tonight, your What-if's, will NEVER come! You have to get the fact that your What-If's are not meant to STOP you, hallelujah, they're meant to DELAY you!!! Somebody say delay! Jonah allowed his What-if's to take root; so much that he began to live life his way. . . . I'm going to buy me a ticket. I'm going to get on this boat. I'm going to go to the bottom of the ship. . . .I'm. . . .I'm . . . I'm. You see when pressure has you on the run, things stop being about God and start being about you. . . . I feel, I think, and so on. I, I, I . . . The enemy does not fear YOU; he fears what's IN YOU! Some of you have been on the run for so long, you have businesses that you're sitting on, inventions still waiting to be made, songs waiting to be written, babies waiting to be born, marriages waiting to be ordained, and doors of opportunities waiting to be opened; all because you're on the RUN! How does a college educated man end up working in sanitation? How does a Christian girl end up selling her body for money? How does a talented child end up in a jail cell? They're on the RUN! Like Jonah went to the bottom of the ship, when you're on the run you wade your way to the bottom of life (living on street corners, working dead-end jobs, hiding out in the shadows of life). You begin to put yourself so far down, because you're afraid of what will happen when others finally begin to see the goodness, the grace, the mercy, and the favor all over your life. When you're at the bottom, you go to sleep on God. When you're sleep, sin becomes habit. That's when lying comes in, fornication begins, jealousy is born, back-biting steps in, that cussing tongue takes root. Why? Because you've fallen asleep. When you're sleep, trouble happens. When you're sleep, all hell breaks loose. But notice in verse 4, where it says, 'But the Lord. .." In all things, 'But the Lord.' In all the hell that I've been through, 'But the Lord. . .,' but God. Psalms 124 tells us, 'Had it not been for the Lord, who was on our side when men rose up against us. . .'. . . But God. . . .But God. I know that this happened to me, but where would I be if the Lord wasn't on my side. In all things, it's but the Lord. When people mistreat you, 'But God.' When you're lied on and talked about, 'But God.' When things don't go according to planned, 'But God.'"

Sitting here listening to the sermon, I feel the weight of every word. God knew that I needed this. I've been trying so hard for so long. At the end of the sermon, it's time for altar prayer. To tell you the truth, my heart feels relieved. When the music plays, the hurting crowd slowly make their way to the altar, and so do I. My legs walk to the altar with a mind of their own. Step by step and tear by tear. As I kneel before the altar, I feel a hand on my shoulder. Turning around, I see that it's Taja, the little girl with no mom. I grab her hand, and together, we kneel before God.

CHAPTER 3

July 21, 2014

Taja

Sometimes it feels best to be alone, so I lock myself in a room listening to the CD player play Nina Simone. Though written a while ago, I feel as if she knows me best. Her lyrics speak the words unspoken in my heart better than the rest. Today's my birthday as you can see, and I'm so excited at what Mrs. Patterson gave me: a Ladies of Jazz cd collection (featuring legends like Nina Simone, Ella Fitzgerald, and Billie Holiday), a microphone, and a keyboard. Never have I had a birthday like this before.

"I ain't got no home, ain't got no shoes, Ain't got no money, ain't got no class. . ."

Knock! Knock!

"Come in." Looking towards the door, I see Mrs. Patterson walking in.

". . . . Ain't got no mother, ain't got no culture, Ain't got no friends, ain't got no schooling, Ain't got no love, ain't got no name, Ain't got no ticket, ain't got no token, ... "

"Well, I see you found your gift."

"Thanks," I reply, smiling from ear to ear.

"Who's that? Nina?"

"Yep."

"Well," she says, sitting next to me on the bed. "I'm glad that you like it. You know before you came, I wouldn't have even thought about coming up here," She admits, looking at me with both joy and pain in her eyes. "This room used to be my boy's room. He was about your age. He liked music, but he loved himself some bowling. His daddy, my husband Robert, used to take him to the bowling alley every Wednesday and Friday night."

Laughing half-heartedly more so to herself than anyone, she continues. "The nearest alley is like 20 or so minutes away as you know. So one night, I spoke with Robert on the phone, and we were arguing about him not having Troy, our son, home because he had a test the very next day. And Robert told me, 'We'll be there in a few.' You see he was mad, because I was making him cut their bowling by like an hour or so. How stupid of me?" Looking down into her hands, the tears begin to roll down her face like a steady stream. "It was raining pretty hard that night. I remember, because I had looked outside a few times and I didn't see them. I tried calling Robert's phone, but it kept going straight to voicemail. And when I heard the doorbell ringing, I just knew that it would be him with some long drown out excuse as to why he hadn't made it in time. But instead, two officers stood at my door. It turns out, Robert and Troy weren't going to make it home that night. They got into an accident; some drunk driver crossed the median and hit them head on. They didn't have a chance." Watching Mrs. Patterson cry, I can feel the pain in her voice and see the regret in her tears. "I blamed myself, for soooooo long . . . had I not been so persistent . . . so demanding. . . . my husband and my son would be here today, standing with me. . ." Unsure of what to do, I put my arms around her. She looks like she's in need of a hug.

As she cries on end, listening to the speakers, I hear the song *'Cry Me A River.'* Listening to Ella's voice, I get lost in my own trace.

"*. . .You drove me, nearly drove me, out of my head, while you never shed a tear. Remember, I remember, all that you said? You told me love was too plebeian. Told me you were through with me, and now you say you love me. Well, just to prove that you do. Come on and cry, cry, cry me a river. . .Cry me a river. I cried, I cried, I cried a river over you. If my pillow talk, imagine what it would have said. Could it be a river of tears I cried instead? Well you can cry me a river. Go ahead and cry me a river. 'Cause I cried, I cried a river over you. . ."*

Sitting up and wiping her eyes, Mrs. Patterson straightens back up to her normal self. "I'm so sorry for breaking down like that. This is really the first time that I've ever discussed this. Anyway, I've said all that to say this. I'm so happy that you're here. Two years ago, I could've never seen myself at this point. It's crazy, because when I got custody of you, I was trying to help you and your situation; but what actually happened, is that over the past few months, you have helped me more than you will ever know. And for that, I say thank you and happy 12th birthday my dear."

We hug yet again. And if I have to say so myself, it's great to finally have a home.

Ding-Dong! Ding-Dong!

Standing up, Mrs. Patterson looks at me, "I wonder who that could be? We're not setting up for the party for another two hours or so."

Ding-Dong! Ding-Dong!

Anxious, we both go down stairs. While Mrs. Patterson goes to answer the door, it's been my intention to try these chocolate cupcakes first-hand. Hearing Mrs. Patterson answer the door, all I can hear her saying is 'No! No! You can't do this!' Going to the door to see what all the commotion is about, I see my momma (for the first time in over 11 months) along with two police officers. With nothing else left, all I hear is *'Cry Me A River'* replaying over and over again in my head:

"...Told me you were through with me, and now you say you love me. Well, just to prove that you do come on and cry me a river. Cry me a river. I cried a river over you..."

****

August 12, 2014

Nicki

I finally got saved, but I still didn't have a place to stay. So the church offered me a room and board if I'd agree to teach the youth. With lodging and food accounted for, this was an offer that I couldn't ignore. So checkered past or not, I'm here every Sunday teaching Sunday school with everything that I've got. Boy, oh boy, my father sure would be proud of me. The church even offered to help me finish my degree. I've never seen people so kind. After inquiring why, I found out that Terrell had put his name on the line. So it's true, when you need it most, God always sends an angel. I just hope that we're both reaching for the same goal.

"Hey, you missed a spot." I look up at Terrell and he's smiling as always.

"I'll go back over it when I finish." Smiling and grinning, I continue to vacuum between the church pews. Seems as if the church was in dire need of a janitor, and since I stay here now, I jumped on the offer. It doesn't pay much, but it does keep some money in my pocket. After giving my life to Christ, the Pastor wanted to make sure that I was clean before giving me the keys to the church, so the church sent me through their twelve step program. Some days are harder than others, but hey it's a start.

"Yeah, yeah, but hey, look what I've got." Looking up, I see him holding a Wendy's bag and two drinks. My Lord, he read my mind. "What do you say? Lunch break?"

"Yeah ok." I turn off the vacuum and we head into the church lodge. We both sit down at the first table available. Biting into my hamburger, I'm completely lost at the fact that Terrell is still staring at me.

"Gee whiz, you can slow down. I'm not going to take it from you I promise." I look up, sort of embarrassed, and we both laugh.

Finally clearing my mouth, I say, "Yeah, ok."

"So talk to me. How's it going?"

Taking another bite of my sandwich, I shrug my shoulders until my mouth becomes clear. "Ummm, well it's going so-so. I mean every day brings different challenges of its own. Some days are good, and some days are not."

"Anything I can do?"

"No, not really. I just feel like this is a fight for me and God; something that's been a long time coming."

"So tell me a little more about you. I feel like I'm getting to know pieces about you at a time, you know."

"Well, what do you want to know?"

"Anything. I mean, where are you from? Is your family living? But most of all, how did you end up here?"

"Well, I'm originally from Philadelphia. I grew up in the church for the most part, St. Elizabeth Chapel."

"St. Elizabeth? That church is big. They're apart of the Western Hill Association. They…"

". . . trade off services with three other mega churches throughout the year, I know."

"Wow, well how did you end up here?"

"Well, it was in the tail end of my senior year in high school, and my family broke apart."

"What happened?"

"Well, my father, Minister Hines, left my mother for the choir director. Just watching how the situation was treated, I mean, the church itself pretty much gave my mom the boot by marrying my father and his mistress, all in like a four month time period. Imagine having all of us at church on Sunday morning, one big happy family," I answered, laughing to myself. "Anyway, he maintained his title and pretty much forgot that we existed. He stopped supporting me financially through school, and by then, I was in my first year at Penn State. And for the longest, I blamed myself for the whole ordeal. It felt like I was the only straw that held my parents together for so long. Anyway, my mom got real sick. She started gagging all the time, losing all kind of weight, and having the hardest trouble catching her breath. She ended up being so depressed and withdrawn that it became pretty hard to get along with her for a while there. So to no surprise, she passed not too long after that. Man said that it was a suicide, but I still say that it was from a broken heart. I guess she just got tired of it all." Feeling the pain all over again, I'm comforted only by the sound of my own tears. My heart wants to cut off the pain and move on with my life as is, but my soul needs this release. So with a deep sigh, I choke up on my thoughts, fears, and emotions, and then continue. "She was all I had. And she was . . . is gone. . . . You know that he had the audacity to come to the funeral offering up his money and time." Again, I laugh half-heartedly to myself. "He still didn't get it. It was never about the money. It was about him. Not really sure how to cope or who to lean on, I left camp and never looked back." I pause for a second, taking time to let the reality of the situation break in. ". . . I spent my whole life trying sooooo hard to meet the expectations and wishes of my parents. I graduated high school at the top of my class. I taught Sunday school with my mom. I went to Penn State majoring in Business Management just like my dad. I dated who they wanted me to date. I went where they wanted me to go. I had so much of life wrapped up in them that when everything fell apart, I did too. . . . You know even up until now whenever I turn on the TV or go online, he's always preaching these hell-bound sermons and half of them be about ME!" I laugh again, more to myself than anything. "I mean he wears that 'prodigal-son,' and the 'enemy-has-you-bound' mess slap out. I know them people get tired of hearing that, because I do. What a joke!"

With my head bent down, I watch as my tears fall from my face onto my pants. He really thinks he's something. It's so crazy how even now, the pain and the hurt still feels real, even after all of these years.

Looking up at Terrell, I don't know whether that's hurt or confusion on his face. Maybe he's like me and finally learned that most things taken to be true are lies. "You know that story about Lot and his family leaving the city."

"Yeah, the angel told them to leave and never look back, but the wife did and she became a pillar of salt."

"Yeah. . .That's how I feel most times. Whenever I think back on what was, I lose sight of what is, and everything in me fades away." Not fully sure of what to do, Terrell gets up and walks over to me. After standing there for a few seconds, probably trying to figure out the best approach, he hugs me. Not like some pity-patter hug, but like one that read 'I-understand.' Yeah, he understands.

CHAPTER 4

October 25, 2014

Taja

It's been three whole months, and I haven't seen Mrs. Patterson yet, seeing as how my momma finally decides to take me back. Just when I finally belonged, just when I finally found peace, here she comes preying on the weak. Since the day that I left a place so peaceful and sound, I haven't heard old man joy come around. I've been called a 'blind-bat,' 'just plain dumb,' and 'just plain stupid.' I've been locked in closets and beaten with sticks. You'd think by now that I'd be used to it. But that's the thing about fairytales, they don't last for long. Seeing as how, my blindness is a gold-mine to the face whose love is no longer mine, all I have on this pilgrim's journey to comfort me is my music, my church, and my sanity.

"Taja." Hearing mom call me from the front seat, I turn up the volume on my CD player. Nina Simone's voice is the only thing that I want to hear right now.

"...Can't you see it? Can't you feel it? It's all in the air. I can't stand the pressure much longer, Somebody say a prayer..."

"Taja!" You can keep calling me, but I'm still not going to answer.

"....Alabama's gotten me so upset. Tennessee made me lose my rest, and everybody knows about Mississippi..."

Momma yanks the headphones from my ears. "Didn't you hear me calling you?"

Not wanting to say 'no' and not willing to say 'yes', I put my head down, pleading the 5th.

Feeling frustrated, momma turns back around and prepares to give me a lecture on what and what not to say. "Look, you better keep your mouth shut today. I don't want any kind of trouble out of you. The only reason that I'm bringing you here is because I'm required to for visitation. I'll pick you up Wednesday night after bible study, and you better be ready. I'm not trying to stay around this place any longer than I have to." As we come to a stop in front of Mt. Calvary, I quickly grab my things; and before she can say another word, I jump out and slam the door behind me.

I'm cutting it pretty close this morning, but I can still make it to youth Sunday school in time enough for breakfast. Reaching the youth room, I grab a pop-tart off of the table and slide into a seat on the back row trying to cause as less commotion as possible.

"Well hello there Taja, we're glad to have you back," exclaims Ms. Nicki. She's been teaching Sunday school for a minute now, and I'm glad that she is. She always brings snacks and prizes.

"Hey."

"Continuing with our decision, Jesus asked the young man whether or not he wanted to be healed. In our lives, we have to 'want' Jesus to come in and make a change. By doing this, we show our faith in Him. Now notice that in the story, this certain blind man had been in this predicament for quite some time. Imagine that you're eating your breakfast, but you can't tell me the color of it. Imagine that you're playing outside, but you can't see the pretty blue sky—"

Ding! Ding!

"Well, that's the church bell. Let's do a closing prayer and then we'll return to the sanctuary. Alright, everyone bow your heads....Dear Lord, we want to..."

As she continues to pray, my mind falls back on the blind man. You see, I've heard this story many times before, but I've never really got it. In the story, all the man had to do was ask, but I've been asking Jesus for my sight for a while now. Can't He hear me? Was I not being good enough? In Sunday school, we've been discussing how Jesus turned water into wine, how He feed the 5,000, how He walked on water, and so on. But if Jesus can do all that, why can't He heal me?

". . . In your son Jesus name we pray, Amen."

As everyone prepares to leave, I take this as an opportunity, so I jet over to Ms. Nicki's desk.

"Hey pretty girl. How are you?" she asks, giving me a hug.

"I'm good. Ms. Nicki, can I talk to you for a minute?"

"Sure sweetie, come on, let's sit down for a minute." Taking a seat in the nearest desks, she asks, "What's on your mind?"

"Did Jesus really do all of those things? You know, like walking on water, turning water into wine, and all of the other stuff?"

Obviously taken aback, Ms. Nicki begins to chuckle a little before gathering herself for an answer. "Yeah sweetie, I believe that he did?"

"Then why can't He heal me?"

No longer smiling, Ms. Nicki touches my hand. "You know, sometimes we ask God for things. Sometimes He says 'yes', sometimes He says 'no', and sometimes He says 'wait'. Whatever He says, it's for the best."

"But how can me being blind in one eye be for my good?"

"Well, Jesus does what He knows to be best. Sometimes, we feel trapped and of no use, but it's in those very times that He uses us best. By crippling you, He in His goodness allowed you to complete others. It's through your blindness that I met you. It's through your blindness that you met Mrs. Patterson, in a time where she needed love the most."

"But momma's taking me away from Mrs. Patterson."

"Ahhhh sugar, I don't think that the story is finished yet, because God has the last say so." We both begin to chuckle in agreement. "Now, are you about ready to go in? I think there's someone waiting to see you."

"Ok." And with that, we're off. As we walk into the sanctuary, I can't help but think that today is going to be a good day. As we reach the pews, the first face that I see is

Mrs. Patterson's. Laying eyes on her, I run up to her and give her a hug. And together, we take our seats in the pews.

***

Nicki

Seeing Taja and Mrs. Patterson during the service makes me feel like true happiness is actually possible. And even though God has not finished working out the situation, I know that He won't stand to see them separated, even with all of the obstacles that her mother continues to throw in the way. Service is just getting started, and it's already off to a great start. After praise and worship, it'll be time for Terrell's part, which is scripture. As the choir sits down, I begin the process of retrieving my bible and head straight for the gospels (even though he knows the word like the back of his hand, he only reads scripture from the gospels; if you can believe that).

"Praise the Lord everybody." The congregation responds. "It's truly an honor to be in the house today, because God is truly up to something. Can I get an Amen?" The congregation responds back. "Well, with that being said, we have a special surprise for you all today. So instead of me doing scripture about Jesus' love, teachings, and forgiveness, I thought that it would be nice to see such things in action. So without further ado, I introduce to some and present to others our guest speaker on today, Minister Hines, all the way from Philadelphia's St. Elizabeth Chapel." Amidst the applause, my mind is running wild. No freaking way! Looking straight at me, Terrell smiles. I'm not exactly sure what he's trying to do, but I'm in no mood to find out.

Lost in my thoughts, I watch aimlessly as the wolf in sheep's clothing takes the mount. "Praise the Lord Saints! Praise the Lord Saints! I say praise the Lord Saints!" He is skinning and grinning as the crowd erupts like he's some local celebrity or something. I tell you, that man still loves to put on a show. "Saints, God's been good. I say that God's been good saints. . ." Not even five minutes into his speech and I'm already tuning him out. I tell you one thing though; he definitely looks like he's lost a few pounds. I guess little Mrs. Prep hasn't quite learned how to cook yet!

". . . Today, I've been asked to speak briefly on 'planting your seeds on good ground' in honor of your annual Harvest Day Celebration." He moves from behind the pulpit to rally the congregation pew by pew, you know to get up close and personal with the crowd to really spur on the Ooh's and Ah's. I swear these people act like he's Jesus walking on water or something. "But after some prayer and a little talk with the Lord, I've been led to speak on a subject that I know best. Can I get an Amen?"

The crowd responds eagerly hanging onto his every word. "Take your time preacher," yells some woman in the congregation.

"Alright now!" Lord, why did she say that? Got this man cruising down the aisle like he's on the red carpet or something.

Feeling this to be a praise break, one musician cracks the drum while the other strikes the guitar. Somebody hits the keyboard, and before you know it, the entire congregation is up dancing . . . everyone, except for me. Watching in agony as this man carries on like he's in some juke (sliding up and down the aisle like Elvis and Michael Jackson mixed together), all I really want to do is get away. While everyone is up dancing, smiling, and clapping, I'm stuck, made to witness this man's foolishness.

As the musicians die down, the poor guy takes a moment to catch his breath. "Oh, hallelujah church! How many of you know that there's no better praise than to dance before the Lord?" The congregation erupts in response yet again. "Oh, what a God we serve church." Turning to the musicians, he queues them to cease, then he continues. "Oh hallelujah saints. Moving right along, how about I bring the word, Amen?" The congregation responds in agreement. "Alright, I'll be coming to you today from Luke 15: 8-10." He gives the congregation time to find the text before continuing. "And it reads. . ."

Seeing that he is now two rows in front of me, it's now or never. Everyone is now standing for the reading, but once the scripture is read, I can make a quick getaway, which sounds good to me. "And we'll stop right here church. According to the text, the woman had 10 coins, in other words it was 10 jewels. It was 10 cherished pieces. When she got up that morning, she had 10 pieces. When she went to work that day, church she still had 10 pieces. But when she went in for the night, she only had 9. The power of this text is not in the fact that the coin was lost. The power of this text comes from the fact that she knew that it was missing! Can I get an Amen? Let us pray. Father God . . ." Already shifting to the end of the row, I'm half way in between my thoughts and my anger. How could Terrell do such a thing? I just know that he had something to do with this. This has his name written all over it. As I stand around anxiously waiting for the prayer to end, I lock eyes with Terrell who's obviously picked my mind, because from where he stands, all he can do is look at me and shake his head 'no.' Sorry Terrell, not this time.

". . . Amen. You may take your seats." That's my cue. At that exact moment, dad turns back toward the pulpit, and I head straight for the door. "My topic today is..."

Bump!

Of all the luck, I'm literally two feet from the door when I bump into an usher on the way to her seat, causing her to drop the fistful of fans that she carries so proudly.

"Oh, I'm so sorry," I say as I do my best to pick up the fans as fast as I can. But judging by the sound of things, it's already too late.

Standing up in the middle of the aisle, all I can see is how my father's eyes are fixed on me. It's like for the first time in almost eight years, he's finally found his missing piece. Obviously scared out of his wits, he once again steps from the pulpit, like he's headed for his own execution. Step by step, he makes it to the middle of the aisle . . . and comes face to face with me. Taking a few seconds to gather his thoughts, he finally gets the urge to speak. "Nickemma? . . ." Speaking with a voice so low, it's like the whole congregation heard the pain of his words, because instead of whooping and hollering, the entire building goes silent. And suddenly I feel as if I'm locked in a room with nobody there but the two of us. And with every second of silence, the chains of my past tighten its grip, purging every single pain out of me.

Seeing the tears on his face, I suddenly begin to notice the tears on mine. Not willing to stay another second, I say the only thing that comes to mind. "It's Nicki!" and out the door I go.

So with that, I'm gone, gone, gone…back into the city streets. This time for good.

CHAPTER 5

November 05, 2014

Nicki

"Hey!" In walks Terrell.

"Hey, yourself." I say, barely looking up from my broom.

"I see that you're getting this place back in tip-top shape."

"Yeah it looks that way," I reply, still sweeping my life away.

Clearly seeing my disinterest, he takes the broom from my hands, ensuring that he has my undivided attention. "Have a seat. I think that you need a break." Seeing as how I still haven't moved, he decides to change his tone. "Please." Now that's more like it. So, slowly but surely we take our seats in the pews. "Ok clearly, you're still upset with me, but please let me explain." With a deep sigh, I prepare myself for what I know I don't want to hear.

"There's nothing to explain."

"But I want to anyway."

Giving in, I say, "Go ahead, shoot."

"I grew up in a family where I was raised by my grandparents. And I didn't even know my father. Here you are, you had a mother and a father. And with your mother gone, it's just you and him, and you guys don't even speak."

"Which clearly has nothing to do with you?"

"Yes it does, more than you know. You go about your life treating people like they're some second hand; always keeping your distance, never letting anyone get too close, and closing yourself off from the world. You live in this box where there's no one but you."

"Oh, so I'm just this bad person. I'm just…"

"No, you're not. You're selfish."

"Excuse me?"

"Face it, you're selfish. You know why you've been floating through life, going from city to city and person to person? Because you don't care to have anybody around. You walk around with this stigma of what you 'think' about men and what you 'think' life is, based on the one man that broke your heart. Now I understand your past and your pain, but that's not God's fault. It's not even your father's fault. It's yours. The fact is, you placed so much faith and value in others, because you didn't want to see the light in yourself. It's not your father who dropped out of college. It's not your father who bailed when your mom died. It's not your father who made you sell yourself night after night for a little pocket change. It's not your father who had you rocking the streets homeless. That was all you."

"Well, I see whose side you're on."

"Nicki, it's not about taking sides. It's about you finally being woman enough to take control of your life.

That's your father. And yes, he's made mistakes, but everyone has. His only job, his only purpose on earth, was to give you life. That's it! So whatever happened after that was because of choices that YOU made." He takes a minute to let his words soak in before continuing in a more sincere voice. "You need to forgive him."

"Forgive him?"

"Yes."

"Why? So he can get off scot-free? It's because of him that I lost my mother. It's because of him that I had to watch as our things were being thrown out into the streets, and we were evicted from our house." Now releasing the tears that I've been wanting to cry for so long, I yell out, "It's because of him. Why don't you see that?"

"You know after you left that Sunday, I stayed after church and talked with him for a little bit. I even apologized for inviting him knowing that you would be there, but do you know what he told me?" I shrug my shoulders, not really caring to hear the answer. But aiming to get his point across, Terrell continues on anyway. "He told me that he wouldn't have had it any other way. Nicki, he's dying."

Shocked by the words that I've just heard, I have to ask a second time. "What?"

"He's dying."

"Dying?" I'm not sure how, but in that exact moment, all of my anger suddenly turns into concern. And for the first time in my life, I pitied him. "Dying of what? Cancer? Diabetes or something?"

"He's dying of AID's."

Hearing the words that have just escaped Terrell's mouth, I gasp trying desperately to catch my breath, but all I catch are my own tears.

Feeling the pain, Terrell grabs my hand, "But Nicki, there's more." Now really confused, I look up at him, not really knowing what to expect. "He told me to tell you."

"Tell me what?"

"A few of weeks before your mother died, she went for a check-up because she wasn't feeling well."

"I remember, she was always so sick. Sometimes, she couldn't even stand."

"Well, uh, when she went to the doctor, she found out that she was HIV positive. Your father had cheated for so long, that he ended up giving his own wife, a saved woman, his problem."

Not really knowing what to do, I cry even harder.

"Your mom couldn't take it. Being a nurse herself, she knew what to expect. So instead, she chose to end it all."

Still crying, it's like my whole life is crashing down in front of me. Holding my hand, Terrell continues, "I think that you should get checked out, seeing as how we're not sure how long either of your parents have had it." He holds my hand even tighter. "I'll go with you if you'd like." Feeling my pain, he hugs me, a comfort that I so desperately need.

***

December 13, 2014
Taja

Standing before the judge for the first time before men, I have to gather the courage to testify in order to navigate my own end. The pressure of having each word carry its own weight is a burden that I've slowly began to hate. How can I choose between this one and that? When really, everyone has both their pros and their cons. Lord, please be with me even on today, because I fully trust you to make a way.

"Please raise your right hand," states the judge in a calm cool sort of way. I raise my hand as instructed. "Do you so solemnly swear to tell the truth and nothing but the truth so help you God?"

"I do."

"Alright, you may take your seat." As I sit in the cushioned black chair, my eyes unconsciously drift down toward my feet. "Now, Ms. Taja." Seeing this as my cue to look up, I do. "Neither Mrs. Patterson nor your mother are permitted to be present during your testimony. Being 12 years of age in the state of New York, that legally gives you the right to choose between either of the two homes presented to you. Are you ready to begin?"

Looking him straight in the eyes, I reply, "Yes sir, I am."

CHAPTER 6

January 01, 2015

Nicki

    Well with a new year comes new changes, or so they say. I ended up testing negative for HIV. Thank you Lord! And by the grace of God, Terrell and I are getting married this coming June. Nothing too fancy, but everyone that I care about is invited. Taja's going to be my flower girl. Jenna's going to be my maid of honor, and yes, she's coming all the way from Chi-town. And my father, Minister Hines, will be giving me away and marrying me off, so I guess I did get the fairytale after all. My dad and I still have our moments, but we're working on it.

    Taja finally got her happily-ever-after as well. She ended up getting adopted by Mrs. Patterson. She's even doing better in school. No, she's not playing sports, but she is back in honor's courses. I'm so proud of her.

    You know, my mom used to tell me all the time that 'when butterflies turn back into caterpillars, they're wings just aren't ready to fly.' I didn't understand what she was talking about then, but I do now. When I entered life on my own, I was the age of a butterfly, but mentally I was still a caterpillar. And with all of the past hurt and pain, my wings weren't strong enough to fly, not then. I had to go back and learn how to crawl first (by learning how to love, how to forgive, how to be myself, and how to be happy), before I could take off and truly be the person that God made me to be. It wasn't easy, but most journeys usually aren't. So thanks mom, you've helped me more than you know.

OTHER BOOKS BY TATIANA WHIGHAM

Do You Know Your Worth?

Lyrics From An Old Soul

www.ingramcontent.com/pod-product-compliance
Lightning Source LLC
Chambersburg PA
CBHW072112290426
44110CB00014B/1895